Cybersecurity Essentials Made Easy
A No-Nonsense Guide to Cyber Security

For Beginners

© All Rights Reserved

This book is the author's original work. References used during the author's research are included in the book. The information contained within it is provided for lawful and ethical purposes only, and the author cannot be held responsible for any inappropriate or unlawful use of the information. Plagiarism and the use of online tools for cheating are strictly prohibited.

Dear Dad,
You were always there for me, supporting and guiding me through every step of my journey. Your love and wisdom will always be with me, and I am so grateful for our time together. I miss you every day, but I know that you are always with me in spirit.

To my dear Wife,
Thank you for being my rock, support, and best friend. Your love and encouragement have meant the world to me, and I am so grateful to have you by my side. I love you with all my heart.

To my Brothers,
Thank you for always being there for me and being such a constant source of support. You have always been true friends, and I am so blessed to have you in my life.

To my Mom,
Thank you for your unwavering love and support. You have always been there for me, and I am so grateful for the guidance and wisdom you have shared with me. I love you more than words can express.

To my Kids,
You are the light of my life and the reason for everything I do. Your love and joy bring me happiness, and I am so blessed to be your Dad. Thank you for being my greatest joy and inspiration.

FOREWORD 6
INTRODUCTION 7
CHAPTER 1- INTRODUCTION TO CYBERSECURITY 8
CHAPTER 2 - CYBERSECURITY FRAMEWORK COMPARISON 14
CHAPTER 3 - RISK ASSESSMENT TOOLS, TECHNIQUES, AND BEST PRACTICES ..16
CHAPTER 4 - PROTECTING YOUR NETWORK AND DEVICES 18
CHAPTER 5 - SAFEGUARDING PERSONAL AND CONFIDENTIAL INFORMATION ...20
CHAPTER 6 - SOCIAL ENGINEERING AND PHISHING ATTACKS 22
CHAPTER 7- CYBERSECURITY FOR REMOTE WORK 24
CHAPTER 8 - MOBILE SECURITY 27
CHAPTER 9 - WEB APPLICATION SECURITY 31
CHAPTER 10 - SECURITY OF THE SUPPLY CHAIN AND THIRD-PARTIES 37
CHAPTER 11 - RESPONDING TO A CYBER ATTACK 40
CHAPTER 12 - REPORTING TO SENIOR MANAGEMENT AND THE BOARD 43
CHAPTER 13 - THE GROWING ROLE OF MACHINE LEARNING IN CYBER 47
CHAPTER 14 - CYBERSECURITY CAREER PATH 54
CHAPTER 15 - CONCLUSION 57
APPENDIX A - EXAMPLES OF CYBER RISKS ACROSS INDUSTRIES 59
REFERENCES: 66

Foreword

Having worked for 25+ years in risk management as a Chief Risk Officer for large financial institutions and a senior risk management advisor for many other companies, I have seen the rise of cyber security risk from a niche risk exposure turn into one of the biggest challenges for businesses. Most risks a company is exposed to, for example, credit risks, have some degree of predictability and can be better modeled by risk managers. If the economy is expected to go through a recession soon, credit defaults would also increase so firms can increase provisions beforehand to weather the storm. In cyber risk, significant issues can happen out of the blue sky and usually are unexpected. They have devastating consequences not just for the companies that suffered a cyber-attack but also for their clients and counterparties and can severely impact a company's reputation. While large corporations can reacquire customer and counterparts' confidence after an incident, this might not be an option for small and mid-sized firms. Today, as most transactions of any kind are done online, businesses are responsible for protecting customer information and their data and information assets.

Cybersecurity threats like viruses, phishing attacks, and social engineering can cause data breaches, financial losses, and the loss of confidential information. This book is intended to give business professionals and small business owners a basic understanding of cybersecurity, including how to protect networks and devices, keep personal and confidential information safe, and respond to cyber-attacks.

With easy-to-understand explanations and practical tips, "Cybersecurity Essentials Made Easy" covers all the essentials of cybersecurity, including cybersecurity tools, cybersecurity risks and controls, and cybersecurity attack and defense strategies.

The book also includes a detailed overview of the cybersecurity career path, with insider tips on landing a job in this exciting field and succeeding once you're there. Plus, a bonus section on the latest data breaches and the role of machine learning in cybersecurity.

I have known Daniel for a long time, and he is one of the leading experts in the industry. He has been a practitioner in cyber security for many years and has led large organizations' information and cyber security teams. Daniel was careful enough to avoid technical jargon and make the difficult and complex issue of cyber security easy to read and understand.

Dr. Marcelo Cruz
Managing Partner, Yacamy Advisors

Introduction

As the business world increasingly relies on technology, cybersecurity has become a crucial concern for businesses of all sizes. Cyber threats can come in many forms, including viruses, malware, phishing attacks, and social engineering. These threats can lead to data breaches, loss of confidential information, and financial damage.

Business professionals need to understand the basics of cybersecurity to protect their organizations and customers. This book aims to provide a comprehensive overview of cybersecurity essentials for business professionals, including best practices for protecting networks and devices, safeguarding personal and confidential information, and responding to cyber-attacks.

I am delighted that you have considered reading my book about cybersecurity. As a business owner or employee, it is essential to have a strong understanding of cybersecurity to protect your organization's sensitive information and prevent costly data breaches. This book will provide a comprehensive overview of the various types of cyber threats and the measures you can take to mitigate them. It will be a valuable resource for you and your organization, and I hope you enjoy it.

Daniel Paula
Chandler, Arizona, December 2022

Chapter 1- Introduction to Cybersecurity

Cybersecurity deals with protecting computer systems, networks, and devices from digital attacks and threats.

Cyber threats can lead to data breaches, loss of confidential information, and financial damage. These threats can come in many forms, including viruses, malware, and phishing attacks.

The importance of cybersecurity for businesses cannot be overstated. In today's digital age, companies of all sizes rely on technology and are, therefore, vulnerable to cyber threats. In fact, according to the 2019 Cost of a Data Breach Report by the Ponemon Institute, the global average cost of a data breach is $3.92 million (Ponemon Institute, 2019). This cost can include legal fees, customer notification, and lost business. In addition to the financial impact, data breaches can damage a company's reputation and customer trust.

It is essential for businesses to understand the types of cyber threats that they may encounter and to take steps to protect themselves. This includes implementing strong security measures, training employees on data protection best practices, and conducting regular data backup and recovery processes.

Businesses may encounter several types of cyber threats, including:

Viruses: Programs designed to replicate themselves and spread from one computer to another. Viruses can cause harm to computer systems and networks by deleting or corrupting files, stealing personal information, and disrupting system functions.

Malware: Malware is a term used to describe any software that is designed to cause harm to a computer system or network. This includes viruses and other types of malicious software such as Trojan horses, worms, and ransomware.

Phishing attacks: A phishing attack is a social engineering attack involving fake websites or emails to trick individuals into revealing personal information. Attackers can use phishing attacks to steal login credentials, financial information, and other sensitive data.

In addition to these types of threats, businesses may also encounter different types of cyber-attacks, such as denial of service (DoS) attacks, where an attacker seeks to make a website or network unavailable to users, and SQL injection attacks, where an attacker injects malicious code into a website's database.

Businesses can implement several security measures to protect against these types of threats. This includes using strong and unique passwords for all accounts and devices, implementing two-factor authentication, keeping software and applications up to date, and using antivirus and malware protection.

In addition to these technical measures, it is also crucial for businesses to train employees on data protection best practices. This includes educating employees on identifying phishing attacks and other types of social engineering and handling sensitive information such as customer data.

Data backup and recovery is another critical aspect of cybersecurity. By regularly backing up data, businesses can ensure they have a copy of important information during a cyber-attack or other disaster.

In recent years, numerous high-profile cyber breaches have significantly impacted organizations and their stakeholders. Some of these cyber breaches and their root causes include:

- Marriott International (2018): A data breach at Marriott International's subsidiary, Starwood Hotels & Resorts, exposed the personal data of up to 500 million guests. The root cause of the breach was the failure to secure an acquired company's systems properly.
- Equifax (2017): A data breach at credit reporting agency Equifax exposed the personal data of 143 million consumers, including names, Social Security numbers, and birth dates. The root cause of the breach was a vulnerability in the company's web application software that the company did not correctly patch.
- Yahoo (2013-2014): A series of data breaches at Yahoo exposed the personal data of all 3 billion of the company's users. The root cause of the breaches was the failure to secure

the company's systems properly, the use of weak passwords, and the lack of encryption for sensitive data.
- Target (2013): A data breach at retail giant Target exposed the personal data of up to 110 million customers, including names, addresses, and credit card numbers. The root cause of the breach was the failure to properly secure the company's network and the lack of segregation between the company's cardholder data environment and the rest of the network.
- Anthem (2015): A data breach at healthcare provider Anthem exposed the personal data of up to 78.8 million customers, including names, Social Security numbers, and medical histories. The root cause of the breach was a vulnerability in the company's web application software that the company did not correctly patch.
- Home Depot (2014): A data breach at home improvement retailer Home Depot exposed the personal data of up to 56 million customers, including names, addresses, and credit card numbers. The root cause of the breach was the failure to properly secure the company's network and the use of weak passwords.
- Sony Pictures (2014): A data breach at Sony Pictures exposed the personal data of up to 47,000 employees and confidential company documents and emails. The root cause of the breach was the failure to properly secure the company's systems and the lack of encryption for sensitive data.
- eBay (2014): A data breach at e-commerce giant eBay exposed the personal data of up to 145 million users, including names, addresses, and passwords. The root cause of the breach was the failure to properly secure the company's systems and the use of weak passwords.
- JP Morgan Chase (2014): A data breach at financial institution JP Morgan Chase exposed the personal data of up to 76 million households and 7 million small businesses. The root cause of the breach was a vulnerability in the company's web application software that the company did not correctly patch.

Research shows that the most critical cybersecurity risks companies face include the following:

1. Data breaches: A data breach is a security incident in which unauthorized individuals gain access to sensitive or confidential information, such as customer data or financial information. Data breaches can result in significant financial losses, reputational damage, and regulatory penalties.
2. Malware attacks: Malware is malicious software designed to harm or exploit vulnerabilities in computer systems. Malware attacks can compromise data, steal sensitive information, or disrupt operations.
3. Phishing attacks: Phishing attacks are a type of cybercrime in which attackers use fake emails or websites to trick users into revealing sensitive information, such as login credentials or financial information. Phishing attacks can be highly effective and result in significant financial losses or data breaches.
4. Ransomware attacks: Ransomware is malware that encrypts a victim's data and demands payment in exchange for the decryption key. Ransomware attacks can result in significant disruption to business operations and can be costly to mitigate.
5. Insider threats are cyber threats from within an organization, such as employees or contractors who have authorized access to the organization's systems and data. Insider threats can be challenging to detect and can significantly damage the organization.
6. Advanced persistent threats (APTs): APTs are sophisticated cyber attacks designed to evade detection and persist in a target system for an extended period. APTs can be highly damaging and result in significant financial losses or data breaches.
7. Cloud security risks: Companies that use cloud-based services to store or process data may face various cybersecurity risks, including data breaches, unauthorized access, and data loss.
8. Internet of Things (IoT) security risks: The increasing number of connected devices in organizations (e.g., smart devices, sensors, and machines) can create additional cybersecurity risks, such as the potential for data breaches or unauthorized access to the devices.
9. Cyber espionage: Cyber espionage refers to using cyber means to gather sensitive or confidential information for competitive or malicious purposes. Cyber espionage can result in significant financial losses and damage the organization's reputation.

10. DDoS attacks (Distributed Denial of Service) attacks involve overwhelming a website or network with traffic to disrupt operations or make it unavailable. DDoS attacks can result in significant disruptions to business operations and can be costly to mitigate.
11. Web application vulnerabilities: Web applications, such as websites and online portals, can be vulnerable to attacks that exploit vulnerabilities in their design or implementation. These attacks can result in data breaches, unauthorized access, or disruption of operations.
12. Network security risks: Companies may face various network security risks, including unauthorized access to networks, data breaches, and disruptions to operations.
13. Mobile security risks: Using mobile devices, such as smartphones and tablets, can create additional cybersecurity risks, such as the potential for data breaches or unauthorized access to devices.
14. Social engineering attacks: Social engineering attacks involve manipulating individuals into revealing sensitive information or taking actions that compromise security. These attacks can be highly effective and result in data breaches or other security incidents.

It is vital for companies to regularly assess their cybersecurity risks and implement appropriate measures to mitigate these risks, such as employee training, security controls, and incident response plans. Such measures include:

1. Data encryption: Encrypting sensitive or confidential data can help protect it from unauthorized access during a data breach.
2. Antivirus and anti-malware software: Installing and regularly updating antivirus and anti-malware software can help detect and prevent malware attacks.
3. Employee training: Providing training on identifying and preventing phishing attacks can help mitigate the risk of these types of attacks.
4. Backups: Regularly backing up data can help organizations recover from a ransomware attack without paying the ransom.

5. Access controls: Implementing strong access controls, such as two-factor authentication, can help prevent unauthorized access to sensitive data and systems by insider threats.
6. Network segmentation: Segmenting networks can help limit the impact of APTs by isolating infected systems and limiting the attackers' access to the rest of the network.
7. Cloud security measures: Implementing security measures, such as encryption and access controls, can help mitigate the risks associated with using cloud-based services.
8. IoT security measures: Implementing security measures, such as encryption and access controls, can help mitigate the risks associated with connected devices.
9. Cyber espionage prevention: Implementing encryption and access controls and training employees on the importance of protecting sensitive information can help prevent cyber espionage.
10. DDoS protection: Implementing network firewalls and intrusion detection systems can help mitigate the risk of DDoS attacks.
11. Web application security measures: Implementing regular patching and vulnerability assessments can help prevent web application vulnerabilities.
12. Network security measures: Implementing firewalls, intrusion detection systems, and network segmentation can help prevent unauthorized network access and data breaches.
13. Mobile device security measures: Implementing device encryption, access controls, and regular updates can help prevent data breaches and unauthorized access to mobile devices.
14. Social engineering prevention: Providing employees with training on identifying and preventing social engineering attacks can help mitigate the risk of these types of attacks.

In conclusion, cybersecurity is a crucial concern for enterprises of all sizes. The financial and reputational costs of a data breach can be significant, and it is essential for companies to understand the types of cyber threats that they may encounter and to take steps to protect themselves. By implementing strong security measures, training employees on data protection best practices, and conducting regular data backup and recovery processes, businesses can help to ensure the security of their systems and data.

Chapter 2 - Cybersecurity Framework Comparison

There are several cybersecurity frameworks that organizations can use to help protect their systems and data.

Some of the most well-known frameworks include:

- NIST Cybersecurity Framework (CSF): Developed by the National Institute of Standards and Technology (NIST), the CSF is a risk-based framework that helps organizations manage and protect their critical assets. Pros: The CSF is widely used and recognized and provides a flexible and adaptable approach to cybersecurity that can be tailored to an organization's specific needs. Cons: It may be complex and time-consuming to implement and require significant resources to maintain.
- ISO 27001: This framework is an international standard that outlines an organization's information security management system (ISMS) requirements. Pros: It is a comprehensive and well-established standard that provides a systematic and structured approach to managing information security. Cons: It can be expensive and time-consuming to implement and requires ongoing maintenance to ensure compliance.
- COBIT: Developed by the Information Systems Audit and Control Association (ISACA), COBIT is a framework for managing and governing information and technology. Pros: It provides a comprehensive and holistic approach to information and technology management and is widely recognized and used. Cons: It can be complex and require significant resources to implement and maintain.
- PCI DSS: The Payment Card Industry Data Security Standard (PCI DSS) is a set of requirements for organizations that handle credit card transactions. Pros: It provides specific and detailed guidance on securing credit card transactions and protecting sensitive data. Cons: It can be costly and time-consuming to implement and maintain,

and non-compliance can result in significant fines and penalties.
- HIPAA: The Health Insurance Portability and Accountability Act (HIPAA) is a federal law that sets standards for protecting health information. Pros: It provides specific and detailed guidance on how to protect sensitive health information. Cons: It can be complex and require significant resources to implement and maintain, and non-compliance can result in significant fines and penalties.

In conclusion, several cybersecurity frameworks are available for organizations to choose from, each with pros and cons. The NIST Cybersecurity Framework (CSF), ISO 27001, COBIT, PCI DSS, and HIPAA are all well-known frameworks widely adopted by organizations worldwide. These frameworks provide a range of approaches to managing and protecting critical assets, information, and technology and can be tailored to meet an organization's specific needs. However, it is important to note that implementing and maintaining these frameworks can be complex and resource-intensive, and non-compliance can result in significant fines and penalties. Therefore, it is important for organizations to carefully consider which framework is most appropriate for their needs and allocate the necessary resources to ensure its successful implementation and ongoing maintenance.

Chapter 3 - Risk assessment tools, techniques, and best practices

Cyber risk assessment is identifying and evaluating the risks to an organization's assets, including its information and systems, from cyber threats. This process helps organizations understand the potential impacts of these threats and the likelihood of them occurring, and it allows them to prioritize their cybersecurity efforts and allocate resources accordingly.

There are various tools and techniques that organizations can use to conduct a cyber risk assessment. Some common tools include

- Risk assessment frameworks: These provide a structured approach for identifying and evaluating risks. Examples include the NIST Cybersecurity Framework and ISO 27001.
- Vulnerability assessment tools scan an organization's systems and networks to identify vulnerabilities that attackers could exploit.
- Threat intelligence platforms: These provide real-time information about emerging threats and help organizations understand the potential impacts of these threats on their systems and data.
- Cybersecurity risk management software: These help organizations manage and prioritize their cybersecurity efforts by providing a centralized platform for storing and analyzing risk assessment data.

In addition to these tools, there are several techniques that organizations can use to conduct a cyber risk assessment, including

- Threat modeling: This involves identifying the assets that are most critical to an organization and analyzing the potential threats to those assets.
- Risk assessment matrix: This grid allows organizations to evaluate the likelihood and potential impact of different risks.
- Business impact analysis: This involves identifying the potential impacts of a cyber incident on an organization's operations and finances.

There are also several best practices that organizations should follow when conducting a cyber risk assessment:

1. Involve relevant stakeholders: It's important to involve a range of stakeholders in the risk assessment process, including IT professionals, business leaders, and legal and compliance teams.
2. Use a risk-based approach: Rather than addressing every potential risk, organizations should prioritize their efforts based on different risks' potential impacts and likelihood.
3. Update regularly: Cyber risks are constantly evolving, so it's important to regularly review and update an organization's risk assessment to ensure it remains relevant and effective.
4. Communicate findings: It's important to communicate the risk assessment results to relevant stakeholders so that they can take appropriate actions to mitigate identified risks.

In conclusion, cyber risk assessment is a critical process for helping organizations understand and manage the risks to their assets from cyber threats. There are various tools and techniques that organizations can use to conduct a risk assessment, including risk assessment frameworks, vulnerability assessment tools, threat intelligence platforms, and cybersecurity risk management software.

Organizations can use threat modeling, risk assessment matrices, and business impact analysis to identify and evaluate the risks to their systems and data. Organizations should involve relevant stakeholders, use a risk-based approach, update their risk assessments regularly, and communicate the findings to relevant parties to ensure the risk assessment process is effective. By following these best practices, organizations can effectively identify and prioritize the risks to their systems and data and take appropriate measures to mitigate them.

Additionally, it is essential to remember that a cyber risk assessment is only as effective as the data and information it is based on, so organizations need to ensure that their assessment is based on accurate and up-to-date information.

By carefully considering these factors and following best practices, organizations can effectively identify and prioritize the risks to their systems and data and take appropriate measures to mitigate them.

Chapter 4 - Protecting Your Network and Devices

As the internet becomes more prevalent in our daily lives, it is vital to ensure the security of our personal and business networks and devices. This chapter will discuss some best practices for password security, the benefits of two-factor authentication, the importance of updating software and applications, and antivirus and malware protection.

Best Practices for Password Security

Passwords are the first defense against cyber threats, so choosing strong, unique passwords for all your accounts is important. Here are some best practices for password security:

- Use letters, numbers, and special characters in your passwords.
- Avoid using personal information in your passwords, such as your name or birthdate.
- Do not reuse passwords for multiple accounts.
- Use a password manager to generate and store unique passwords for each account.
- Enable two-factor authentication, which we will discuss in more detail later, for added security.

Two-Factor Authentication

Two-factor authentication (2FA) is an additional security layer requiring a second form of authentication beyond just a password. This could be a code sent to your phone, a biometric scan, or a physical token. 2FA helps to prevent unauthorized access to your accounts, even if someone has your password. Enable 2FA on all your accounts, especially those containing sensitive information, such as financial accounts or email, is a good idea.

Updating Software and Applications

Keeping your software and applications up to date is essential for several reasons. First, updates often include security patches that fix vulnerabilities in the software. Cybercriminals can exploit these vulnerabilities to gain access to your device or network. By installing updates, you can help protect yourself against these threats.

In addition to security patches, updates may include new features or improvements to the software. By keeping your software and applications up to date, you can ensure that you are getting the best performance and user experience.

Anti-Virus and Malware Protection

Antivirus and malware protection are crucial for protecting your devices and network from malicious software.

Antivirus software scans your device for known viruses and removes them if detected. Malware protection helps to prevent the installation of malware, which can include viruses, worms, and ransomware.

It is vital to keep your antivirus and malware protection software up to date to ensure that it is effective at protecting your device. You should also be cautious when downloading files or visiting websites to reduce the risk of malware infection.

In conclusion, protecting your network and devices is essential in today's digital age. By following best practices for password security, enabling two-factor authentication, keeping your software and applications up to date, and using antivirus and malware protection, you can help to keep your device and network secure.

Chapter 5 - Safeguarding Personal and Confidential Information

In the digital age, personal and confidential information is often stored and shared electronically, making it important to protect it from cyber threats. This chapter will discuss best practices for protecting customer data, handling sensitive emails and documents, and data backup and recovery.

Protecting Customer Data

Customer data is a valuable asset for businesses, and it is crucial to protect it from unauthorized access or breaches. Here are some best practices for protecting customer data:

- Implement strong security measures, such as two-factor authentication and encryption, to prevent unauthorized access.
- Regularly update software and applications to fix vulnerabilities and protect against cyber threats.
- Conduct regular security audits and assessments to identify and address any potential weaknesses in your systems.
- Follow data privacy laws and regulations, such as the General Data Protection Regulation (GDPR) in the European Union or the California Consumer Privacy Act (CCPA) in the United States.

Handling Sensitive Emails and Documents

Emails and documents containing sensitive information, such as financial or personal data, should be handled with extra care to prevent unauthorized access or leaks. Here are some best practices for managing sensitive emails and documents:

- Use encryption to protect the contents of the email or document.

- Use secure methods for sharing and transferring sensitive information, such as secure file-sharing platforms or encrypted messaging apps.
- Follow company policies and procedures for handling sensitive information.
- Regularly review and update access controls to ensure that only authorized individuals can access sensitive information.

Data Backup and Recovery

Data backup and recovery are essential for protecting against data loss due to cyber threats or hardware failures. Here are some best data backup and recovery practices:

- Regularly back up your data to a secure location, such as an external hard drive or cloud storage.
- Test your data backups regularly to ensure that they are working correctly.
- Have a disaster recovery plan to guide you through restoring your data in case of a breach or hardware failure.
- Use data backup and recovery software to automate and protect your data.

In conclusion, safeguarding personal and confidential information is essential in the digital age. By following best practices for protecting customer data, handling sensitive emails and documents, and implementing data backup and recovery measures, you can help to ensure the security of your and your customer's sensitive information.

Chapter 6 - Social Engineering and Phishing Attacks

Social engineering and phishing attacks are tactics used by cybercriminals to trick individuals into revealing sensitive information or performing actions that compromise security. This chapter will discuss social engineering, the types of social engineering attacks, and how to identify and prevent phishing attacks.

What is Social Engineering?

Social engineering uses psychological manipulation to influence individuals to reveal sensitive information or perform actions that compromise security. These attacks often rely on the trust and goodwill of the victim, as well as their tendency to follow social norms or authority figures.

Types of Social Engineering Attacks

There are various social engineering attacks, including

- Phishing attacks involve sending fake emails or websites that appear legitimate but are designed to trick individuals into revealing sensitive information or downloading malware.
- Impersonation attacks involve an attacker pretending to be someone else, such as a colleague or customer, to obtain sensitive information or gain access to systems.
- Scareware attacks involve tricking individuals into believing their device is infected with malware and prompting them to purchase fake software to fix the problem.
- Baiting attacks involve offering a reward or incentive in exchange for sensitive information or access to systems.

How to Identify and Prevent Phishing Attacks

Phishing attacks are one of the most common forms of social engineering, so it is important to be able to identify and prevent them. Here are some tips for identifying and preventing phishing attacks:

- Be wary of emails or websites that request sensitive information, such as passwords or financial information.
- Verify the authenticity of emails or websites by checking the sender's email address and the website's URL.
- Use antivirus and malware protection software to help detect and prevent phishing attacks.

A phishing attack typically involves the following steps:

- The attacker creates a fake email or website that appears legitimate, often by impersonating a trusted organization or individual.
- The attacker sends the fake email or directs the victim to the phony website, often using tactics such as urgency or fear to prompt the victim to take action.
- The victim enters their sensitive information, such as passwords or financial information, into the fake email or website, believing it to be legitimate.
- The attacker uses the victim's sensitive information for nefarious purposes, such as stealing their identity or accessing their accounts.

In conclusion, social engineering and phishing attacks are common tactics used by cybercriminals to trick individuals into revealing sensitive information or compromising security. By being aware of these tactics and taking steps to identify and prevent them, you can help protect yourself and your organization from these threats.

Chapter 7- Cybersecurity for Remote Work

The COVID-19 pandemic has significantly shifted towards remote work, with many companies and organizations transitioning to a fully or partially remote workforce. While remote work can bring many benefits, it introduces new cybersecurity risks and challenges. This chapter will explore best practices for remote work, protecting company data on personal devices, and using virtual private networks (VPNs) to enhance cybersecurity for remote workers.

Best Practices for Remote Work

Remote work can be vulnerable to cybersecurity threats due to the lack of physical security and the use of personal devices for work purposes. Organizations need to implement best practices for remote work to minimize the risk of cyber attacks.

1. Use strong, unique passwords and enable two-factor authentication: Strong, unique passwords are essential for protecting accounts and data from unauthorized access. Two-factor authentication (2FA) adds a layer of security by requiring a second form of authentication, such as a code sent to a phone or email, before granting access to an account.

2. Keep software and devices up to date: Regularly updating software and devices can help prevent attackers from exploiting vulnerabilities. This includes updating operating systems, antivirus software, and applications.

3. Use secure communication channels: To protect sensitive data, it is essential to use secure communication channels, such as encrypted email or messaging tools, when communicating with colleagues or clients.

4. Use secure networks: Remote workers should use secure networks, such as a VPN, when accessing company resources. This helps to protect data from being intercepted by third parties.

5. Enable remote wipes for company devices: If a device is lost or stolen, it is crucial to have the ability to remotely wipe company data from the device to prevent unauthorized access.

Protecting Company Data on Personal Devices

As more employees are using personal devices for work purposes, organizations need to implement measures to protect company data on these devices.

- Use device management solutions: Device management solutions allow organizations to enforce security policies on personal devices, requiring strong passwords and enabling remote wipes.
- Encrypt data: Encrypting data can help prevent unauthorized access if a device is lost or stolen.
- Implement separation of work and personal data: To prevent accidental sharing of company data, it is important to implement solutions that separate work and personal data on personal devices.

Virtual Private Networks (VPNs)

A virtual private network (VPN) is a secure network connection that allows remote workers to access company resources as if they were on the company's internal network. VPNs can help to enhance cybersecurity by encrypting data transmitted between the device and the company's network, protecting it from interception by third parties.

There are several types of VPNs, including

- Remote-access VPNs: Remote-access VPNs allow remote workers to access company resources from their devices securely.
- Site-to-site VPNs: Site-to-site VPNs connect two networks, such as a company's headquarters and a branch office, over the internet.
- Mobile VPNs: Mobile VPNs allow mobile devices, such as smartphones and tablets, to access company resources securely.

To use a VPN, a remote worker must first install VPN software on their device and then connect to the company's VPN server. Once connected, all data transmitted between the device and the company's network is encrypted, providing an additional layer of security.

In conclusion, the shift towards remote work has introduced new cybersecurity risks and challenges. To minimize these risks, organizations must implement best practices for remote work, such as using strong passwords and enabling two-factor authentication, keeping software and devices up to date, using secure communication channels, and enabling remote wipes for company devices. Protecting company data on personal devices is crucial through device management solutions, encryption, and separation of work and personal data. The use of virtual private networks (VPNs) can also enhance cybersecurity for remote workers by encrypting data transmitted between the device and the company's network. Organizations can effectively protect their data and minimize cybersecurity risks in a remote work environment by implementing these measures.

Chapter 8 - Mobile Security

Mobile devices, such as smartphones and tablets, have become integral to our daily lives. They provide a convenient and portable way to access the internet, communicate with others, and store and access personal and confidential information. However, as our reliance on mobile devices increases, so does the risk of mobile security threats. This chapter will explore the various types of mobile security threats, best practices for protecting mobile devices, and tips for safeguarding personal and confidential information.

Introduction to Mobile Security

Mobile security refers to the measures taken to protect mobile devices and their data from unauthorized access, misuse, or loss. Mobile security is important because mobile devices are vulnerable to various security threats, including malware, phishing attacks, and physical theft. These threats can result in the loss or theft of sensitive information, such as login credentials, financial data, and personal identification, as well as the disruption of services and the potential for financial loss.

Types of Mobile Security Threats

There are several types of mobile security threats that can affect mobile devices:

1. Malware: Malware is software designed to perform malicious actions on a device, such as stealing sensitive information or disrupting services. Types of malware include viruses, worms, and Trojan horses.
2. Phishing attacks: Phishing attacks are attempts to trick users into revealing sensitive information, such as login credentials or financial data, through fake websites or emails that appear legitimate.
3. Physical theft: Mobile devices are vulnerable to physical theft, which can result in the loss of sensitive data and the potential for financial loss.

4. Unsecured networks: Connecting to unsecured networks, such as public Wi-Fi, can expose mobile devices to cyber threats, as data transmitted over these networks are vulnerable to interception by third parties.

Best Practices for Protecting Mobile Devices

To protect mobile devices from security threats, it is essential to follow best practices, including:

1. Use strong, unique passwords: Strong, unique passwords can help prevent unauthorized access to mobile devices.
2. Enable security features, such as screen locks and biometric authentication, can help prevent unauthorized access to mobile devices.
3. Keep software and apps up to date: Regularly updating software and apps can help prevent attackers from exploiting vulnerabilities.
4. Use a mobile security app or service: Mobile security apps or services can help to detect and prevent security threats on mobile devices.
5. Avoid connecting to unsecured networks: To protect data from being intercepted by third parties, it is essential to avoid connecting to unsecured networks, such as public Wi-Fi, unless using a VPN.
6. Enable remote wipe: If a mobile device is lost or stolen, it is crucial to have the ability to remotely wipe company data from the device to prevent unauthorized access.

Keeping Software and Apps Up to Date

Keeping software and apps up to date is essential to mobile device security. Software and app updates often include security patches that fix vulnerabilities that attackers could exploit. It is necessary to regularly check for and install updates to ensure that mobile devices are protected against the latest security threats.

Enabling Security Features such as Screen Locks and Biometric Authentication

Security features, such as screen locks and biometric authentication, can help prevent unauthorized access to mobile devices. Screen locks, such as passcodes or patterns, require users to enter a code before accessing the device. Biometric authentication, such as fingerprint scanners or facial recognition, uses unique physical characteristics, such as fingerprints or facial features, to verify the user's identity. These security features add layer protection to mobile devices and can help prevent unauthorized access.

Using a Mobile Security App or Service

Mobile security apps or services can help to detect and prevent security threats on mobile devices. These apps or services often include antivirus protection, phishing protection, and the ability to locate or wipe a lost or stolen device remotely. It is essential to carefully research and choose a reputable mobile security app or service to ensure the best protection for mobile devices.

How to Respond to a Lost or Stolen Mobile Device

Suppose a mobile device is lost or stolen. In that case, it is crucial to take immediate action to prevent unauthorized access to the device and its data. Steps to take include:

1. Report the loss or theft to the authorities, if applicable.
2. Change any passwords associated with the device and accounts accessed on the device.
3. Use the remote wipe feature, if available, to erase the data from the device.
4. Cancel any credit cards or accounts linked to the device, if applicable.

Tips for Protecting Personal and Confidential Information on Mobile Devices

To protect personal and confidential information on mobile devices, it is essential to follow these tips:

1. Use strong, unique passwords for all accounts accessed on the device.
2. Enable security features, such as screen locks and biometric authentication.
3. Use a mobile security app or service to detect and prevent security threats. Be cautious when downloading apps and only download from reputable sources.
4. Avoid connecting to unsecured networks, such as public Wi-Fi, unless using a VPN.

Conclusion: Mobile devices have become an integral part of our daily lives. Still, they are also vulnerable to a variety of security threats. To protect mobile devices and the data stored on them, it is important to follow best practices, such as using strong passwords, enabling security features, and keeping software and apps up to date. In case of a lost or stolen mobile device, it is crucial to take immediate action to prevent unauthorized access to the device and the stored data. Mobile security apps or services can also provide an additional layer of protection. Following these steps and tips, individuals can protect their mobile devices and safeguard personal and confidential information.

Chapter 9 - Web Application Security

Web applications, such as online shopping sites, social media platforms, and banking systems, play a critical role in our daily lives. They provide convenient and easy access to various services and information. However, as our reliance on web applications increases, so does the risk of web application security threats. This chapter will explore the various types of web application security threats, best practices for protecting web applications, and tips for safeguarding personal and confidential information.

Introduction to Web Application Security

Web application security refers to the measures taken to protect web applications and their data from unauthorized access, misuse, or loss. Web application security is vital because web applications are vulnerable to various security threats, including cross-site scripting (XSS), SQL injection attacks, and cross-site request forgery (CSRF). These threats can result in the loss or theft of sensitive information, such as login credentials, financial data, and personal identification, as well as the disruption of services and the potential for financial loss.

Types of Web Application Security Threats

There are several types of web application security threats that can affect web applications:

1. Cross-site scripting (XSS): XSS attacks involve injecting malicious code into a web application, which is then executed by the browser of the user visiting the web application. This can result in the theft of sensitive information or the execution of malicious actions.
2. SQL injection attacks: SQL injection attacks involve injecting malicious code into a web application through input fields, such as login forms or search bars. The database then executes the injected code, potentially allowing the attacker to access or modify sensitive data.

3. Cross-site request forgery (CSRF): CSRF attacks involve tricking users into performing unintended actions on a web application, such as transferring funds or changing personal information.
4. Unsecured networks: Connecting to unsecured networks, such as public Wi-Fi, can expose web applications to cyber threats, as data transmitted over these networks are vulnerable to interception by third parties.

Best Practices for Protecting Web Applications

To protect web applications from security threats, it is essential to follow best practices, including:

1. Keep software and apps up to date: Regularly updating software and apps can help prevent attackers from exploiting vulnerabilities.
2. Write secure code: Writing secure code involves following best practices for coding, such as input validation and sanitization, to prevent vulnerabilities in the web application.
3. Enable security features: Security features, such as the secure sockets layer (SSL) and transport layer security (TLS), can help protect data transmitted between the web application and the user's browser.
4. Use web application firewalls (WAFs): WAFs can help detect and prevent security threats on web applications, such as XSS and SQL injection attacks.
5. Avoid connecting to unsecured networks: To protect data from being intercepted by third parties, it is essential to avoid connecting to unsecured networks, such as public Wi-Fi, unless using a VPN.

Keeping Software and Apps Up to Date

Keeping software and apps up to date is essential to web application security. Software and app updates often include security patches that fix vulnerabilities that attackers could exploit. It is vital to regularly check for and install updates to ensure that web applications are protected against the latest security threats.

Writing Secure Code

Writing secure code involves following best practices to prevent vulnerabilities in web applications. Some best practices for writing secure code include:

1. Input validation and sanitization: Validating and sanitizing input can help prevent vulnerabilities like SQL injection attacks. This involves checking that input meets specific criteria, such as being in the correct format and removing or encoding any potentially harmful characters.
2. Escaping output: This can help prevent vulnerabilities like XSS attacks. This involves converting potentially harmful characters into harmless equivalents so that they are not interpreted as code by the browser.
3. Using secure coding frameworks: Secure coding frameworks, such as the Open Web Application Security Project (OWASP) Top 10, provide guidelines and best practices for writing secure code.

Enabling Security Features such as Secure Sockets Layer (SSL) and Transport Layer Security (TLS)

Security features, such as secure sockets layer (SSL) and transport layer security (TLS), can help protect data transmitted between the web application and the user's browser. SSL and TLS use encryption to secure the data transmitted between the two parties, preventing third parties from intercepting and reading the data. Engineering teams can enable these security features by obtaining an SSL or TLS certificate and installing it on the web server.

Using Web Application Firewalls (WAFs)

Web application firewalls (WAFs) can help detect and prevent security threats on web applications, such as XSS and SQL injection attacks. WAFs can be configured to detect and prevent specific types of threats, such as known vulnerabilities or attack patterns. WAFs analyze incoming traffic to the web application and block any malicious traffic.

How to Conduct a Web Application Security Assessment

Conducting a web application security assessment involves identifying and evaluating the security of a web application. Security teams can do this through various methods, including manual, automated, and penetration testing.

Web applications have become a crucial part of modern businesses and organizations, allowing them to interact with customers, partners, and employees through the internet. However, increasing reliance on web applications comes with an increased risk of security breaches, which can have significant consequences for the organization and its users. Therefore, it is essential to take appropriate measures to ensure the security of web applications. This chapter will explore how to conduct a web application security assessment and provide tips for protecting personal and confidential information on web applications.

A web application security assessment systematically evaluates a web application's security posture, intending to identify vulnerabilities and weaknesses that attackers could exploit. There are several approaches to conducting a web application security assessment, including manual and automated testing.

Manual testing involves manually examining the web application and its underlying code and infrastructure to identify potential vulnerabilities. This can be done by an individual or a team of security professionals who use various tools and techniques to assess the web application's security.

Automated testing involves using specialized software to scan the web application and identify potential vulnerabilities. Security teams can configure these tools to scan for various vulnerabilities, including common web application vulnerabilities such as SQL injection, cross-site scripting (XSS), and cross-site request forgery (CSRF).

When conducting a web application security assessment, it is crucial to focus on the following areas:

1. Input validation involves examining how the web application handles user input to ensure it is properly sanitized and validated. Attackers can often exploit vulnerabilities in input validation to inject malicious code or manipulate the application's behavior.
2. Authentication and authorization: This involves examining the web application's mechanisms for verifying user identity and granting access to protected resources. This includes examining the strength of passwords, the implementation of multi-factor authentication, and the use of role-based access controls.
3. Session management: This involves examining how the web application manages user sessions, including the use of cookies and session tokens. Attackers can often exploit vulnerabilities in session management to gain unauthorized access to the application or to steal sensitive information.
4. Data protection: This involves examining how the web application protects sensitive data, including the use of encryption, secure transmission protocols, and secure storage mechanisms.
5. Infrastructure security: This involves examining the underlying infrastructure that supports the web application, including servers, networking equipment, and cloud environments. This includes examining the operating system's security, the configuration of firewalls and intrusion detection systems, and using secure protocols such as HTTPS.

Tips for Protecting Personal and Confidential Information on Web Applications

There are several steps organizations and individuals can take to protect personal and confidential information on web applications. Some key measures include

1. Implementing strong authentication and authorization controls: This includes using strong passwords and implementing multi-factor authentication to verify user identity. It also involves implementing role-based access controls to ensure that users only have access to the resources they need to perform their job duties.

2. Ensuring the security of personal data: This involves using encryption to protect sensitive data in transit and at rest and implementing secure storage mechanisms to prevent unauthorized access to data. It also implements robust data protection policies and procedures, regularly reviewing and updating access controls and monitoring for unusual activity.
3. Protecting against common web application vulnerabilities involves implementing measures to prevent common web application vulnerabilities, such as SQL injection and XSS.

In conclusion, web application security is critical for protecting organizations and their users from cyber threats. Regular security assessments and implementing appropriate controls can help identify and mitigate potential vulnerabilities. Some key measures to safeguard personal and confidential information on web applications include implementing strong authentication and authorization controls, ensuring the security of personal data, and regularly updating software and security protocols. It is also crucial for organizations to educate their employees on best practices for web application security and to have a plan in place for responding to security breaches.

Chapter 10 - Security of the Supply Chain and Third-Parties

Supply chain security and third-party cyber risks are significant concerns for organizations today. Cyber threats can originate from anywhere along the supply chain, and third parties may not have the same security controls as the organization itself. This chapter will explore relevant cyber threats, risks, and mitigating controls in the context of supply chain security and third-party cyber risks.

Cyber Threats in the Supply Chain

There is a range of cyber threats that can originate from within the supply chain, including:

1. Malware is malicious software that malicious actors can introduce into an organization's systems through the supply chain. This may include viruses, worms, Trojan horses, and ransomware.

2. Insider threats may include employees or contractors who intentionally or unintentionally introduce cyber threats into an organization's systems through the supply chain.

3. Intellectual property theft may occur when suppliers or other third parties access and steal confidential information, such as trade secrets, through the supply chain.

4. Unsecured devices, such as USB drives or laptops, can introduce cyber threats into an organization's systems through the supply chain.

Organizations may also face risks from third parties, including:

1. Lack of security controls: Third parties may not have the same security controls as the organization itself, increasing the risk of a cyber breach.

2. Limited visibility: Organizations may have limited visibility into the security practices of third parties, making it challenging to identify and address potential risks.

3. Dependence on third parties: Organizations may be heavily dependent on third parties for specific functions or services, increasing the potential impact of a cyber breach.

Mitigating Controls for Supply Chain Security and Third-Party Cyber Risks

There are several strategies organizations can use to mitigate the risks of supply chain security and third-party cyber risks, including:

1. Conducting thorough due diligence: Organizations should conduct thorough due diligence on potential suppliers and third parties to ensure they have appropriate security controls. This may include reviewing their security policies, conducting assessments and audits, and obtaining references.

2. Implementing security controls: Organizations can implement security controls to protect against cyber threats that may originate from the supply chain or third parties. This may include implementing network segmentation, access controls, and intrusion detection systems.

3. Establishing contracts and agreements: Organizations should develop contracts and agreements with suppliers and third parties that clearly outline their security responsibilities and the consequences of a breach.

4. Training and awareness: Organizations should provide training and awareness to employees and contractors on the importance of supply chain security and third-party cyber risks and the measures in place to protect against these risks.

5. Conducting regular assessments and audits: Organizations should conduct regular assessments and audits to ensure that their supply chain security and third-party cyber risk controls are adequate and up-to-date.

Supply chain security and third-party cyber risks are significant concerns for organizations today. Cyber threats can originate from anywhere along the supply chain, and third parties may not have the same security controls as the organization itself. By conducting thorough due diligence, implementing security controls, establishing contracts and agreements, providing training and awareness, and conducting regular assessments and audits, organizations can effectively mitigate these risks and protect against potential cyber threats.

Chapter 11 - Responding to a Cyber Attack

Cyber attacks have become a significant concern for organizations of all sizes as the frequency and sophistication of these attacks continue to increase. A cyber attack can have serious consequences, including financial loss, damage to reputation, and legal liabilities. Therefore, organizations need to plan to respond to a cyber attack.

This chapter will examine the steps organizations should take in a cyber attack, the importance of incident response planning, and how to recover from a cyber attack.

Steps to take in the event of a cyber attack:

1. Contain the attack: The first step in responding to a cyber attack is to contain and prevent it from spreading further. This may involve disconnecting affected systems from the network, shutting down servers, or isolating the attack.

2. Identify the scope and nature of the attack: The next step is to identify the scope and nature of the attack. This may involve analyzing logs, network traffic, and other data to determine how malicious actors carried out the attack and what systems and data have been compromised.

3. Notify relevant parties: Depending on the severity of the attack and the potential consequences, it may be necessary to notify appropriate parties such as law enforcement, regulatory authorities, and insurance providers.

4. Implement damage control measures: Once the attack has been contained and the scope and nature of the attack have been identified, the organization should implement measures to minimize the damage caused by the attack. This may involve restoring affected systems from backups, implementing patches or updates to fix vulnerabilities, or taking other steps to secure the affected systems.

5. Communicate with stakeholders: The organization needs to communicate with employees, customers, and partners about the attack and the steps to address it. This may involve issuing press releases, updating social media accounts, or holding town hall meetings.

Importance of incident response planning:

Incident response planning prepares for and responds to cyber-attacks or other security incidents. A well-defined incident response plan is critical for any organization, as it helps ensure that the appropriate steps are taken promptly to minimize the impact of an attack.

There are several benefits to having an incident response plan in place:

1. Reduces downtime: A well-defined incident response plan can help minimize downtime by providing a clear set of steps to follow during an attack. This can help reduce the disruption to business operations and prevent the attack from spreading further.
2. Improves communication: An incident response plan helps ensure that all relevant parties are notified in the event of an attack. Clear lines of communication are established. This can help prevent confusion and ensure everyone is working towards a common goal.
3. Minimizes damage: By following an incident response plan, organizations can take the necessary steps to mitigate the damage caused by an attack and reduce the impact on stakeholders.
4. Demonstrates compliance: In some cases, law or industry regulations may require an incident response plan. Organizations can demonstrate compliance and avoid potential fines or legal liabilities by having a plan.
5. Enhances reputation: Responding to a cyber attack effectively can help protect an organization's reputation and prevent damage to its brand. This can be especially important in industries where trust is critical, such as banking or healthcare.

How to recover from a cyber attack:

1. Identify and fix the root cause of the attack: To prevent future attacks, it is essential to identify and fix the root cause of the

attack. This may involve patching vulnerabilities, improving security controls, or enhancing user education and awareness.

2. Restore systems from backups: One of the first steps in recovering from a cyber attack is to restore affected systems from backups. This can help prevent data loss and minimize the disruption to business operations. It is essential to ensure that backups are regularly updated and stored in a secure location to ensure that they are available in the event of an attack.

3. Implement patches and updates: After restoring affected systems, it is crucial to implement patches and updates to fix vulnerabilities that malicious actors may have exploited in the attack. This can help prevent future attacks and ensure that systems are secure.

4. Review and update security measures: The recovery process should also include reviewing the organization's security measures to identify any weaknesses or areas for improvement. This may involve implementing new security technologies, strengthening password policies, or increasing employee awareness and training.

5. Communicate with stakeholders: It is essential to communicate with stakeholders about the attack and the steps being taken to recover from it. This may involve issuing press releases, updating social media accounts, or holding town hall meetings to provide transparency and demonstrate the organization's commitment to protecting its stakeholders.

Cyber attacks are a severe threat to organizations of all sizes. By taking the appropriate steps to contain the attack, identify its scope and nature, notify relevant parties, implement damage control measures, and communicate with stakeholders, organizations can minimize the impact of an attack and recover more effectively. Additionally, having a well-defined incident response plan can help organizations respond more effectively and efficiently to a cyber attack. Organizations must prioritize cyber security and continuously review and update their incident response plan to ensure they are prepared to respond to cyber-attacks.

Senior Management can use several cybersecurity metrics to measure the effectiveness of an organization's cybersecurity efforts. Some of the most important ones include the following:

1. Number and severity of cyber threats: Tracking the number and severity of cyber threats can indicate the organization's overall cybersecurity posture. This may include metrics such as the number of phishing attempts, malware infections, and other types of cyber threats.
2. Vulnerability management: Tracking metrics related to vulnerability management, such as the number of vulnerabilities discovered and the time it takes to patch them, can help organizations identify areas for improvement and ensure that their systems are secure.
3. Cybersecurity incident response time: This metric measures how long it takes for an organization to respond to a cybersecurity incident, from when it is detected to when it is resolved. A shorter response time is generally considered more effective, as it allows an organization to minimize the impact of the incident.
4. Mean time to detect (MTTD): This metric measures how long it takes for an organization to see a cyber attack or security breach. A shorter MTTD is generally more effective, as it allows an organization to respond to the threat more quickly and minimize the attack's impact.
5. Mean time to respond (MTTR): This metric measures how long an organization responds to a detected cyber attack or security breach. A shorter MTTR is generally more effective, as it allows an organization to take more timely and appropriate action to mitigate the threat.
6. Compliance: Organizations may be subject to various cybersecurity regulations and standards. Tracking metrics related to compliance, such as the percentage of systems compliant with these regulations and standards, can help organizations ensure that they are meeting their obligations.
7. User awareness and training: Ensuring that employees are aware of cybersecurity risks and how to protect against them is critical for the organization's overall security. Tracking metrics such as the number of employees who have completed cybersecurity training or the percentage of employees who pass

Chapter 12 - Reporting to Senior Management and the Board

In today's increasingly digital world, cybersecurity has become a top priority for organizations of all sizes. Senior Management and the Board are crucial in overseeing an organization's cybersecurity governance and risk management. Therefore, cybersecurity professionals must communicate effectively with these stakeholders about cybersecurity risks and incidents and the overall performance of the organization's cybersecurity efforts.

Let's examine the importance of keeping senior Management and the Board informed about cybersecurity, how to present cybersecurity information to these stakeholders, and the Board's role in overseeing cybersecurity governance and risk management.

Importance of keeping senior Management and the Board informed about cybersecurity:

1. Cybersecurity is a business risk: Cybersecurity risks can have severe consequences for an organization, including financial loss, damage to reputation, and legal liabilities. Therefore, senior Management and the Board need to be aware of these risks and the measures being taken to mitigate them.
2. Cybersecurity is a Board responsibility: In many cases, the Board has a legal obligation to oversee the organization's cybersecurity governance and risk management efforts. By keeping the Board informed about cybersecurity, cybersecurity professionals can help ensure that the Board is fulfilling this obligation and can provide guidance and direction as needed.
3. Cybersecurity affects stakeholders: Cybersecurity risks and incidents can impact stakeholders such as employees, customers, and partners. By keeping senior Management and the Board informed about these risks and incidents, cybersecurity professionals can help ensure that the organization is taking appropriate steps to protect these stakeholders.

cybersecurity awareness tests can help organizations gauge the effectiveness of their training efforts.

Best practices to present cybersecurity information to Senior Management and the Board:

1. Use clear, concise language: When presenting cybersecurity information to Senior Management and the Board, it is essential to use clear, concise language. Avoid using technical jargon or acronyms that may not be familiar to these stakeholders.
2. Provide context: When presenting cybersecurity information to senior Management and the Board, it is crucial to provide context. This may involve explaining the significance of specific metrics or the potential consequences of a cyber incident.
3. Use visuals: Visual aids such as charts, graphs, and diagrams can help present cybersecurity information clearly and concisely.
4. Practice, Practice, Practice!

Best practices for communicating cybersecurity risks and incidents to senior Management and the Board:

1. Develop a communication plan: Having a communication plan in place can help ensure that relevant stakeholders are notified promptly in the event of a cyber incident. The plan should outline the steps to inform stakeholders and the information to be provided.
2. Use multiple channels: In a cyber incident, it is essential to use various channels to communicate with stakeholders. This may include email, phone, social media, and other channels.
3. Provide regular updates: It is crucial to update Senior Management and the Board about the progress of the incident response and recovery efforts. This can help keep these stakeholders informed and provide reassurance that the organization is taking appropriate steps to address the incident.
4. Be transparent: It is essential to communicate with Senior Management and the Board about cybersecurity risks and incidents. This can help build trust and demonstrate the organization's commitment to protecting its stakeholders.

5. Provide recommendations: When communicating with Senior Management and the Board, it is helpful to provide guidance for addressing cybersecurity risks and incidents. This may include suggestions for improving the organization's cybersecurity posture or addressing specific risks or incidents.

The role of the Board in overseeing cybersecurity governance and risk management entails the following priorities:

1. Set strategic direction: The Board plays a crucial role in setting the strategic direction for the organization's cybersecurity efforts. This may include establishing goals and objectives for the organization's cybersecurity posture and identifying the resources needed to achieve these goals.
2. Review and approve policies and procedures: The Board should review and approve the organization's cybersecurity policies and procedures to ensure they are effective and aligned with its overall risk management strategy.
3. Monitor and assess performance: The Board should monitor and evaluate the organization's cybersecurity performance on an ongoing basis to ensure that it meets its goals and objectives. This may involve reviewing metrics such as the number and severity of cyber threats, incident response time, and compliance with regulations and standards.
4. Provide guidance and direction: The Board should provide guidance and direction to the organization's cybersecurity professionals to help ensure that the organization's cybersecurity efforts are aligned with the overall risk management strategy.

Effective communication between cybersecurity professionals, Senior Management, and the Board is critical for an organization's security. By keeping these stakeholders informed about cybersecurity risks and incidents and the overall performance of the organization's cybersecurity efforts, cybersecurity professionals can help ensure that the organization is taking appropriate steps to protect itself and its stakeholders. The Board oversees the organization's cybersecurity governance and risk management efforts. It is essential for cybersecurity professionals to communicate effectively with the Board to ensure that these efforts are aligned with the organization's overall risk management strategy.

Chapter 13 - The Growing Role of Machine Learning in Cyber

In recent years, there has been a growing interest in using machine learning for cybersecurity. Machine learning is a subset of artificial intelligence that involves the development of algorithms that can learn from data and make decisions or predictions without being explicitly programmed to do so. In the cybersecurity context, practitioners can use machine learning to improve the effectiveness of cybersecurity systems by allowing them to learn from data and adapt to new threats, automate specific tasks, and identify patterns of suspicious activity.

However, there are also potential vulnerabilities and privacy concerns associated with using machine learning in cybersecurity. In this chapter, we will examine how machine learning can help improve cybersecurity systems, how cyber professionals can automate specific tasks, the vulnerabilities of machine learning systems to attacks, and the privacy concerns associated with using machine learning in cybersecurity.

There are several key considerations to keep in mind when discussing the growing role of machine learning in cybersecurity:

1. Machine learning can improve the effectiveness of cybersecurity systems by allowing them to learn from data and adapt to new threats. This can be especially useful for detecting and mitigating emerging threats, such as zero-day vulnerabilities or advanced persistent threats.
2. Security teams can use machine learning to automate certain tasks, such as identifying and blocking malicious traffic or identifying patterns of suspicious activity. This can free cybersecurity professionals to focus on more complex tasks and improve the efficiency of the overall cybersecurity system.
3. Machine learning algorithms can be biased, just like humans. It is crucial to ensure that the data used to train machine learning models is representative and free from bias. If the data used to train the model is biased, the model's predictions and decisions may also be biased.

4. Machine learning models can be complex and difficult to interpret, making it challenging to understand how they arrived at a particular decision or prediction. This can be a concern in cybersecurity, as machine learning systems' decisions can have serious consequences.
5. Machine learning systems are vulnerable to attacks and can be exploited by adversaries. It is crucial to consider the security of machine learning systems and design them with security in mind to protect against attacks.
6. Machine learning systems can generate a large amount of data, which can present privacy concerns. It is important to consider how this data is collected, stored, and used to ensure that privacy is protected.

How machine learning can help improve cybersecurity systems

One of the main ways machine learning can help improve cybersecurity systems is by allowing them to learn from data and adapt to new threats. Traditional cybersecurity systems rely on predefined rules or signatures to identify and mitigate threats. However, these systems can be ineffective against emerging threats, such as zero-day vulnerabilities or advanced persistent threats, as they do not have the necessary rules or signatures to detect and mitigate them.

On the other hand, machine learning algorithms can learn from data and adapt to new threats. These algorithms can be trained on large datasets of both benign and malicious activity, allowing them to learn the characteristics of both types of activity. Once trained, teams can use the algorithms to identify and mitigate new threats by detecting patterns or deviations from regular activity.

One example of machine learning for cybersecurity is intrusion detection systems (IDS). IDS monitors network activity and identifies potential threats, such as malicious traffic or unauthorized access attempts. Traditional IDS rely on predefined rules or signatures to identify threats, but sophisticated adversaries can bypass these systems. On the other hand, data scientists can train machine learning algorithms to identify patterns of suspicious activity and can adapt to new threats as they emerge.

Several types of machine learning algorithms can be used for cybersecurity, including supervised learning algorithms, unsupervised learning algorithms, and semi-supervised learning algorithms. Supervised learning algorithms require labeled training data, including benign and malicious activity examples. The algorithm is then trained to classify new activity instances as benign or malicious based on the characteristics of the training data. Unsupervised learning algorithms do not require labeled training data and instead rely on the algorithm to identify patterns or clusters in the data. Semi-supervised learning algorithms are a combination of supervised and unsupervised learning algorithms and can be used when there is a limited amount of labeled training data available.

How cybersecurity teams use machine learning to automate specific tasks

Cyber teams can also use machine learning to automate specific tasks, such as identifying and blocking malicious traffic or identifying patterns of suspicious activity. Automating these tasks can free cybersecurity professionals to focus on more complex tasks. It can improve the efficiency of the overall cybersecurity system.

One example of the use of machine learning for task automation in cybersecurity is the use of email filters. Traditional email filters rely on predefined rules or keywords to identify and block spam or phishing emails. However, these systems can be bypassed by sophisticated adversaries who use techniques such as domain spoofing or subject line variations to evade detection. On the other hand, engineers can train machine learning algorithms to identify patterns of suspicious activity in emails.

Vulnerabilities of machine learning systems to attacks

While machine learning can be a powerful tool for improving cybersecurity, it is essential to consider the vulnerabilities of machine learning systems to attacks. Adversaries can potentially exploit these vulnerabilities to bypass machine learning-based cybersecurity systems or to manipulate their decisions.

One potential vulnerability of machine learning systems is the use of biased or unrepresentative data to train the model. If the data used to train the model is biased, the model's predictions and decisions may also be biased. For example, a machine learning model trained on a predominantly male dataset may be more likely to classify males as a specific type of user, leading to biased predictions. It is vital to ensure that the data used to train machine learning models is representative and free from bias.

Another vulnerability of machine learning systems is their complexity and lack of interpretability. Many machine learning algorithms are complex and difficult to interpret, making it challenging to understand how they arrived at a particular decision or prediction. This can be a concern in cybersecurity, as machine learning systems' decisions can have serious consequences. For example, a machine learning algorithm that identifies and blocks malicious traffic could block legitimate traffic if it makes an incorrect decision.

Designing machine learning systems with security in mind to address these vulnerabilities and regularly test and evaluate their performance is crucial. Additionally, it may be necessary to incorporate additional measures, such as human oversight or decision-making, to mitigate the risks associated with machine learning in cybersecurity.

Privacy concerns with machine learning systems

The use of machine learning in cybersecurity can also raise privacy concerns, particularly regarding the large amounts of data that machine learning systems can generate. Machine learning algorithms rely on data to learn and make decisions, and this data can include sensitive personal information. It is important to consider how this data is collected, stored, and used to ensure that privacy is protected.

One way to address privacy concerns is through de-identification or anonymization techniques, which involve removing or obscuring identifying information from the data. This can help protect the privacy of individuals while still allowing the data to be used for machine-learning purposes. However, it is important to note that de-identification techniques are not foolproof, and it is possible for adversaries to re-identify individuals through advanced techniques.

Another way to address privacy concerns is through data minimization techniques, which only collect and use the minimum amount of data necessary to achieve the desired result. This helps reduce the amount of data generated and stored, reducing the risk of data breaches or unauthorized access to sensitive information.

Machine learning in cyber attack prevention

One key area where machine learning is being applied in cybersecurity is preventing cyber attacks. ML engineers and data scientists can train machine learning algorithms to recognize patterns of behavior indicative of an impending attack and alert cybersecurity professionals or automatically take preventive measures to mitigate the attack.

For example, practitioners can use machine learning algorithms to detect and block phishing attacks by analyzing emails' content and identifying patterns characteristic of phishing emails. Similarly, practitioners can use machine learning algorithms to detect and block malicious traffic by analyzing network traffic and identifying patterns indicative of an attack.

Machine learning in cyber threat intelligence

Another area where machine learning is applied in cybersecurity is cyber threat intelligence. Cyber threat intelligence involves collecting, analyzing, and disseminating information about current and emerging cyber threats. Practitioners can use machine learning algorithms to analyze large amounts of data and identify patterns or trends that can help inform cyber threat intelligence efforts.

For example, practitioners can use machine learning algorithms to analyze social media data and identify indicators of compromise or malicious activity. Similarly, practitioners can use machine learning algorithms to analyze network traffic data and identify patterns of suspicious activity that may indicate an ongoing cyber attack.

Machine learning in vulnerability management

Machine learning is also applied in vulnerability management, which involves identifying, prioritizing, and mitigating vulnerabilities in a network or system. Practitioners can use machine learning algorithms to analyze data about vulnerabilities and prioritize them based on their potential impact and the likelihood of being exploited.

For example, practitioners can use machine learning algorithms to analyze data about known vulnerabilities and prioritize them based on the potential risk they pose to an organization. This can help cybersecurity professionals prioritize their efforts and focus on mitigating the most critical vulnerabilities first.

Machine learning in cybersecurity incident response

Machine learning is also being applied in cybersecurity incident response, which involves identifying, responding to, and mitigating the impact of cybersecurity incidents. Practitioners can use machine learning algorithms to analyze data about cybersecurity incidents and identify patterns or trends that can help inform incident response efforts.

For example, practitioners can use machine learning algorithms to analyze data about past cybersecurity incidents and identify patterns that may indicate an ongoing or imminent attack. This can help cybersecurity professionals respond more effectively to incidents and mitigate their impact.

Limitations and challenges of machine learning in cybersecurity

While machine learning can improve cybersecurity significantly, it has limitations and challenges. One limitation is the need for large amounts of data to train machine learning algorithms. In cybersecurity, obtaining sufficient data to train machine learning algorithms can take time and effort, particularly for emerging or low-frequency threats.

Another challenge is the potential for machine learning algorithms to be biased or to make incorrect decisions. As mentioned earlier, ensuring that the data used to train machine learning algorithms is representative and free from bias is essential. However, it is still possible for machine learning algorithms to make incorrect decisions, mainly if they need to be adequately trained or if they encounter unexpected data.

In conclusion, using machine learning in cybersecurity can improve the effectiveness of cybersecurity systems and automate specific tasks. By designing machine learning systems with security in mind and addressing privacy concerns, it is possible to leverage the power of machine learning for cybersecurity purposes effectively. However, it is crucial to consider the potential vulnerabilities of machine learning systems to attacks and the privacy concerns associated with using machine learning in cybersecurity.

Chapter 14 - Cybersecurity Career Path

Cybersecurity is a growing and dynamic field that offers a range of career opportunities for individuals with the right skills and knowledge. In this chapter, we will explore the various career paths available in cybersecurity, provide insider tips on how to land a job in this field, and discuss strategies for success once you're there.

An Overview of the Cybersecurity Career Path,

The cybersecurity career path is diverse. It includes a wide range of roles, from technical positions, such as security analysts and engineers, to management roles, such as chief security officers (CSOs) and directors of security. Some individuals may start their careers in entry-level positions, such as security analysts, and then move to more senior roles. Others may choose to specialize in a particular area of cybersecurity, such as network security or digital forensics.

Regardless of their specific role, professionals in the cybersecurity field are responsible for protecting an organization's systems, networks, and data from cyber threats. This may involve monitoring networks for signs of intrusion, developing and implementing security policies and procedures, and conducting security assessments and audits.

Insider Tips for Landing a Job in Cybersecurity

If you're interested in pursuing a career in cybersecurity, there are a few key steps you can take to increase your chances of landing a job in this field:

1. Get an education: A degree in a field such as Computer Science, cybersecurity, or information technology is often preferred by employers in the cybersecurity field. Additionally, obtaining professional certifications, such as the Certified Information Systems Security Professional (CISSP) or Certified Ethical Hacker (CEH), can help demonstrate your expertise and increase your marketability.
2. Build your skills and experience: In addition to formal education, it's important to build practical skills and experience in cybersecurity. This may involve participating in internships or co-

op programs, volunteering for security-related projects, or completing online courses or boot camps.
3. Network: Building relationships with professionals in the cybersecurity field can be a great way to learn about job opportunities and get your foot in the door. Consider joining professional organizations, attending networking events, and participating in online communities to connect with others in the field.
4. Show your passion: Employers in the cybersecurity field are often looking for candidates who are passionate about this field and are committed to staying up-to-date with the latest developments and technologies. Consider sharing your passion for cybersecurity in your resume and cover letter, and be prepared to discuss it in job interviews.

Strategies for Success in a Cybersecurity Career

Once you've landed a job in cybersecurity, there are a few key strategies you can use to succeed in this field:

- Stay current: The cybersecurity field is constantly evolving, so it's crucial to stay up-to-date with the latest technologies, threats, and best practices. This may involve participating in professional development opportunities, such as training courses and conferences, or obtaining additional certifications.
- Build your skills: In addition to staying current, it's important to build and enhance your cybersecurity skills continually. This may involve learning new technologies or techniques or seeking opportunities to take on additional responsibilities or projects.
- Network and collaborate: Building relationships and collaborating with others in the cybersecurity field can help you learn from your peers, identify new opportunities, and stay connected to the latest developments in the field.
- Communicate effectively: As a cybersecurity professional, Leadership may call you upon to explain complex technical concepts to various audiences, including non-technical stakeholders. Developing strong communication skills, including the ability to present complex information clearly and concisely, is crucial for success in this field.

- Understand the business: In addition to technical skills, it's essential for cybersecurity professionals to understand the business needs and goals of the organization they work for. This can help them align their work with the company's overall objectives and ensure that security measures are practical and efficient.
- Be proactive: Cybersecurity professionals should take a proactive approach to their work rather than simply reacting to threats as they arise. This may involve conducting regular assessments and audits, implementing preventative measures, and developing contingency plans in case of a security breach.
- Take on leadership roles: As you gain experience and expertise in cybersecurity, consider taking on leadership roles within your organization or community. This may involve mentoring colleagues, participating in industry groups, or presenting at conferences and events.

The cybersecurity career path offers a range of exciting and rewarding opportunities for individuals with the right skills and knowledge. By obtaining an education, building your skills and experience, networking, and demonstrating your passion for this field, you can increase your chances of landing a job in cybersecurity. Once you're in this field, it's essential to stay current, build your skills, network and collaborate, communicate effectively, understand the business, be proactive, and take on leadership roles to succeed and advance in your career.

Chapter 15 - Conclusion

Thank you for reading this book on cybersecurity essentials for business professionals. We hope you have gained a greater understanding of cybersecurity's importance and the measures you can take to protect your organization and customers from cyber threats.

Throughout the book, we have covered a wide range of topics related to cybersecurity, including an introduction to the field, an overview of common cyber threats, and best practices for protecting networks and devices. We have also discussed the importance of safeguarding personal and confidential information and guided how to respond to cyber-attacks.

One key takeaway from this book is the importance of ongoing cybersecurity awareness and training. As the business world becomes increasingly reliant on technology, all employees must be knowledgeable about cyber threats and how to protect against them. This includes staying up-to-date on the latest threats and best practices and learning about new technologies and tools that can help improve cybersecurity.

In addition to ongoing training, businesses can take several other measures to improve their cybersecurity posture. These include implementing strong passwords and password management protocols, regularly patching and updating software and systems, and maintaining a robust firewall and intrusion detection system. It is also essential to have a plan to respond to cyber attacks, including procedures for preserving evidence, communicating with stakeholders, and recovering from the incident.

Several resources are available if you want to learn more about cybersecurity and continue your education on this topic. Some options include online courses, cybersecurity conferences and events, and professional certifications such as the Certified Information Systems Security Professional (CISSP). You can also stay informed about the latest cybersecurity trends and threats by subscribing to industry publications or following cybersecurity experts on social media.

In conclusion, cybersecurity is a critical concern for businesses of all sizes in today's digital age. Companies can safeguard their systems, data, and customers from harm by understanding the basics of cybersecurity and implementing effective measures to protect against cyber threats. We hope that this book has provided a solid foundation for your cybersecurity knowledge and that you will continue to build upon it as you navigate the ever-changing landscape of cyber threats.

Appendix A - Examples of Cyber Risks Across Industries

Cyber Risks in Technology Firms

Several cybersecurity risks are particularly relevant for Technology firms. Here are some examples, along with appropriate controls to mitigate the risks:

1. Data breaches can result in the loss or theft of sensitive customer data, such as financial or personal identifying information. To mitigate this risk, eCommerce and Technology firms should implement strong security measures, such as firewalls, encryption, and secure password policies. They should also regularly review and update their security protocols to stay ahead of emerging threats.

2. Malware attacks: Malware attacks can compromise the security of a company's systems and networks, potentially leading to data loss or theft. To mitigate this risk, eCommerce and Technology firms should use antivirus software, keep their systems and software up to date with the latest security patches, and train employees to recognize and avoid suspicious emails or links.

3. Phishing attacks involve sending fake emails or texts that appear to be from a legitimate source to trick users into divulging sensitive information or installing malware. To mitigate this risk, eCommerce and Technology firms should educate employees about the signs of phishing attacks and provide them with tools to verify the authenticity of emails and links before they click on them.

4. Denial of Service (DoS) attacks involve flooding a website or network with traffic to make it unavailable to users. To mitigate this risk, eCommerce and Technology firms should use firewalls, intrusion detection systems, and load balancing to ensure their systems can withstand high traffic levels.

5. Insider threats: Insider threats can occur when employees, contractors, or other insiders intentionally or accidentally compromise the security of a company's systems or data. To mitigate this risk, eCommerce and Technology firms should implement strict access controls, regularly review and monitor

employee access to sensitive systems and data, and provide employees with training on security best practices.

It is important to note that the specific controls needed to mitigate these risks will depend on the particular circumstances of the eCommerce or Technology firm. These companies must adopt a comprehensive, multi-layered approach to cybersecurity that combines technical controls with employee training and awareness programs.

Cyber Risks in Government Organizations

Government institutions face a variety of cybersecurity risks, including:

1. Malware and ransomware attacks involve using malicious software to gain unauthorized access to systems or to hold data hostage until a ransom is paid. Controls to mitigate these risks include:

    - Installing and maintaining up-to-date antivirus and anti-malware software
    - Implementing strong passwords and using two-factor authentication
    - Regularly updating and patching software and operating systems.
    - Educating employees on how to recognize and avoid phishing attacks
    - Regularly backing up data to ensure that security teams can recover it in the event of an attack.

2. Insider threats involve employees or contractors with authorized access to systems but use that access for malicious purposes. Controls to mitigate these risks include:

    - Implementing strict access controls and monitoring systems for privileged users
    - Conducting background checks on employees and contractors
    - Implementing security awareness training for employees
    - Establishing policies and procedures for reporting suspicious activity

3. Network attacks: These attacks involve the unauthorized access or compromise of a government institution's network. Controls to mitigate these risks include:

    - Implementing strong network security measures, such as firewalls and intrusion detection systems
    - Regularly updating and patching network devices.
    - Conducting regular security assessments and penetration testing
    - Implementing secure remote access solutions

4. Social engineering attacks: These attacks involve the use of psychological manipulation to trick individuals into divulging sensitive information or performing actions that may compromise security. Controls to mitigate these risks include:

    - Providing security awareness training to employees on how to recognize and avoid social engineering attacks
    - Implementing strict policies and procedures for handling sensitive information
    - Establishing a process for reporting suspicious activity

5. Physical security breaches involve unauthorized access to physical facilities or systems, such as through theft or tampering. Controls to mitigate these risks include:

    - Implementing strict access controls for physical facilities, such as security guards and identification badges
    - Ensuring that all physical systems are adequately secured and monitored
    - Conducting regular security assessments of physical facilities

In terms of importance, it is difficult to rank these risks as each can have significant consequences for a government institution. Government institutions need to have robust controls in place to mitigate all of these risks.

Cyber Risks in Financial Institutions

There are several cybersecurity risks that financial institutions should be aware of and take steps to mitigate. Here are some of the most relevant risks and controls:

1. Malware: Malware is a type of software that is designed to infiltrate or damage computer systems. Malicious actors can spread it through email attachments, infected websites, or other means. To mitigate this risk, financial institutions should implement robust antivirus and anti-malware software and regularly update and patch their systems.

2. Phishing attacks involve using fake emails or websites to trick individuals into divulging sensitive information, such as login credentials or financial data. To mitigate this risk, financial institutions should educate employees on recognizing and reporting phishing attacks and implement email filtering and spam-blocking tools.

3. Insider threats: Insider threats refer to the risk of unauthorized access or misuse of information by an individual within an organization. This can include employees, contractors, or others accessing the organization's systems. Financial institutions should implement strong password policies and access controls to mitigate this risk and regularly monitor and audit employee access to sensitive data.

4. Network security refers to the measures taken to protect an organization's computer networks from unauthorized access, attacks, or other threats. To mitigate this risk, financial institutions should implement firewalls, virtual private networks (VPNs), and other network security measures to protect against external threats.

5. Data breaches refer to the unauthorized access or disclosure of sensitive information, such as customer data or financial records. To mitigate this risk, financial institutions should implement strong security measures, such as encryption, to protect against data breaches and have the plan to detect and respond to any data breaches that occur quickly.

In terms of importance, all of these risks are significant and should be taken seriously. Financial institutions should prioritize implementing controls that address the most severe and likely risks first while also taking steps to address all relevant risks.

Cyber Risks in Healthcare Organizations

The healthcare industry faces a unique set of cybersecurity risks due to the sensitive nature of the information it handles and the potential consequences of a security breach. Some of the most relevant risks include:

1. Data breaches can occur when unauthorized individuals gain access to protected healthcare information, such as patient records or financial data. Controls to mitigate this risk include implementing strong password policies, using two-factor authentication, regularly updating and patching systems, and training employees on security best practices.

2. Insider threats: Insider threats refer to actions taken by employees, contractors, or other insiders who have access to an organization's systems and data. Controls to mitigate this risk include implementing strict access controls, monitoring employee activity, and training employees on how to identify and report suspicious activity.

3. Ransomware attacks involve malware that encrypts an organization's data and demands payment in exchange for the decryption key. Controls to mitigate this risk include regularly backing up data, implementing robust security protocols, and training employees to identify and prevent ransomware attacks.

4. Phishing attacks: Phishing attacks involve the use of fake emails or websites to trick individuals into revealing sensitive information or downloading malware. Controls to mitigate this risk include implementing robust email security protocols, training employees on identifying phishing attacks, and using software to detect and prevent such attacks.

In terms of importance, data breaches are likely the most significant risk facing the healthcare industry, as they can result in the loss of sensitive patient information and financial damages. Insider threats and ransomware attacks are substantial risks that can seriously affect healthcare organizations. While still a significant risk, phishing attacks may be less damaging than these other threats.

Cyber Risks in Fintech

There are several cybersecurity risks that Fintechs should be aware of and take steps to mitigate. Here are some of the most relevant risks and controls:

1. Data breaches: One of the biggest risks in the fintech industry is the potential for data breaches, which can lead to the theft of sensitive financial information and loss of customer trust. To mitigate this risk, fintech companies should implement strong password policies, regularly update software and security systems, and use encryption for data transmission. They should also invest in incident response plans and employee training to ensure that any potential breaches are promptly detected and addressed.

2. Phishing attacks: Another significant risk for fintech companies is the threat of phishing attacks, in which hackers use fake emails or websites to trick users into providing sensitive information. To prevent these attacks, fintech companies should implement two-factor authentication, educate employees on how to recognize and avoid phishing attacks, and use anti-phishing software.

3. Malware attacks: Malware attacks, in which hackers infect computers or devices with malicious software, can also pose a significant risk to fintech companies. To mitigate this risk, fintech companies should regularly update their anti-virus software, use firewalls to prevent unauthorized access, and educate employees on safe internet practices.

4. Insider threats: Insider threats, in which employees or contractors accidentally or intentionally compromise company security, can also be a concern for fintech companies. To mitigate this risk, fintech companies should implement strict access controls, conduct background checks on employees and contractors, and regularly review and update their security policies.

In terms of importance, data breaches are the most significant cybersecurity risk for the fintech industry, followed by phishing attacks, malware attacks, and insider threats.

References:

Chapter 1

Ponemon Institute (2019). 2019 Cost of a Data Breach Report. Retrieved from https://www.ibm.com/security/data-breach

"Data breach statistics." (2021). Ponemon Institute. Retrieved from https://www.ponemon.org/data-breaches

"What is malware?" (n.d.). Symantec. Retrieved from https://www.symantec.com/security-center/threat-glossary/malware

"Phishing attacks." (n.d.). US-CERT. Retrieved from https://www.us-cert.gov/ncas/tips/ST04-014

"Ransomware attacks." (n.d.). US-CERT. Retrieved from https://www.us-cert.gov/ncas/tips/ST04-021

"Insider threats." (n.d.). US-CERT. Retrieved from https://www.us-cert.gov/ncas/tips/ST04-016

"Advanced persistent threats (APTs)." (n.d.). US-CERT. Retrieved from https://www.us-cert.gov/ncas/tips/ST05-002

"Cloud security risks." (n.d.). US-CERT. Retrieved from https://www.us-cert.gov/ncas/tips/ST05-007

"Internet of Things (IoT) security risks." (n.d.). US-CERT. Retrieved from https://www.us-cert.gov/ncas/tips/ST05-011

"Cyber espionage." (n.d.). US-CERT. Retrieved from https://www.us-cert.gov/ncas/tips/ST06-002

Chapter 2

Department of Health and Human Services. (n.d.). HIPAA overview. Retrieved from https://www.hhs.gov/hipaa/for-professionals/index.html

Information Systems Audit and Control Association. (n.d.). COBIT overview. Retrieved from https://www.isaca.org/cobit

International Organization for Standardization. (n.d.). ISO 27001 overview. Retrieved from https://www.iso.org/standard/45170.html

National Institute of Standards and Technology. (n.d.). NIST Cybersecurity Framework (CSF) overview. Retrieved from https://www.nist.gov/cybersecurity-framework

Payment Card Industry Security Standards Council. (n.d.). PCI DSS overview. Retrieved from https://www.pcisecuritystandards.org/pci_security/

Chapter 3

National Institute of Standards and Technology. (2020). Cybersecurity Framework. Retrieved from https://www.nist.gov/cybersecurity-framework

International Organization for Standardization. (2013). ISO/IEC 27001:2013 - Information technology -- Security techniques -- Information security management systems -- Requirements. Retrieved from https://www.iso.org/standard/54599.html
ISACA. (2021). COBIT. Retrieved from https://www.isaca.org/cobit

Payment Card Industry Security Standards Council. (2021). Payment Card Industry Data Security Standard. Retrieved from https://www.pcisecuritystandards.org/pci_security/

Department of Health and Human Services. (2021). Health Insurance Portability and Accountability Act (HIPAA). Retrieved from https://www.hhs.gov/hipaa/index.html

Chapter 4

"Password Security: Tips for Creating and Managing Strong Passwords." Federal Trade Commission. https://www.consumer.ftc.gov/articles/0347-password-security-tips.

"Two-Factor Authentication: What You Need to Know." Stay Safe Online. https://staysafeonline.org/stay-safe-online/protect-your-personal-information/two-factor-authentication/.

"Why is Updating Software Important?" Norton. https://www.norton.com/en/internet-security-center/online-safety/why-is-updating-software-important.

"Anti-Virus and Malware Protection." Stay Safe Online.

https://staysafeonline.org/stay-safe-online/protect-your-personal-information/anti-virus-and-malware-protection/

Chapter 5

"5 Tips for Protecting Customer Data." Small Business Administration. https://www.sba.gov/blogs/5-tips-protecting-customer-data.

"How to Securely Share Sensitive Information." Stay Safe Online. https://staysafeonline.org/stay-safe-online/protect-your-personal-information/how-to-securely-share-sensitive-information/.

"Data Backup and Recovery." Stay Safe Online. https://staysafeonline.org/stay-safe-online/protect-your-personal-information/data-backup-and-recovery/

Chapter 6

"What is Social Engineering?" Stay Safe Online. https://staysafeonline.org/stay-safe-online/avoid-threats/social-engineering/

"Types of Social Engineering Attacks." Stay Safe Online. https://staysafeonline.org/stay-safe-online/avoid-threats/social-engineering/types-of-social-engineering-attacks/.

"How to Protect Yourself from Phishing Attacks." Federal Trade Commission. https://www.consumer.ftc.gov/articles/how-protect-yourself-phishing-scams

Chapter 7

"The Benefits and Challenges of Remote Work." (n.d.). Retrieved from https://www.themuse.com/advice/the-benefits-and-challenges-of-remote-work

"Cybersecurity Best Practices for Remote Workers." (n.d.). Retrieved from https://www.cisco.com/c/en/us/solutions/collateral/enterprise-networks/enterprise-network-security/white-paper-c11-741490.html

"Virtual Private Network (VPN)." (n.d.). Retrieved from https://www.techopedia.com/definition/5019/virtual-private-network-vpn

Chapter 8

"Mobile Security." (n.d.). Retrieved from https://www.symantec.com/security-center/topic/mobile-security

"Mobile Security: Protecting Your Smartphone or Tablet." (n.d.). Retrieved from https://www.us-cert.gov/ncas/tips/ST04-014

"What is Mobile Security?" (n.d.). Retrieved from https://www.trendmicro.com/vinfo/us/security/definition/mobile-security

Chapter 9

OWASP. (n.d.). Web Application Security Testing. Retrieved from https://www.owasp.org/index.php/Web_Application_Security_Testing

NIST. (2014). Guide to Protecting the Confidentiality of Personally Identifiable Information (PII). Retrieved from https://nvlpubs.nist.gov/nistpubs/SpecialPublications/NIST.SP.800-122.pdf

SANS Institute. (n.d.). Tips for Protecting Personal Information. Retrieved from https://www.sans.org/security-awareness-training/tips/

Symantec. (2017). Responding to a Data Breach: A Practical Guide. Retrieved from https://www.symantec.com/content/dam/symantec/docs/white-papers/responding-to-a-data-breach-a-practical-guide-white-paper.pdf

Chapter 10

National Institute of Standards and Technology. (2021). Supply Chain Risk Management Practices for Federal Information Systems and Organizations. Retrieved from https://csrc.nist.gov/publications/detail/sp/800-161/final

Australian Cyber Security Centre. (2021). Supply Chain Cyber Security. Retrieved from https://www.cyber.gov.au/acsc/view-all-acsc-publications/supply-chain-cyber-security

SANS Institute. (2021). Supply Chain Cybersecurity: Five Steps for Mitigating Risk. Retrieved from https://www.sans.org/reading-room/whitepapers/bestprac/supply-chain-cybersecurity-five-steps-mitigating-risk-38496

Chapter 11

"Cybersecurity and Infrastructure Security Agency (CISA) - Incident Response." U.S. Department of Homeland Security, 2021, https://www.cisa.gov/incident-response.

"Incident Response Plan (IRP)." National Institute of Standards and Technology, 2021, https://csrc.nist.gov/publications/detail/sp/800-61/rev-2/final.

"Incident Response Planning." SANS Institute, 2021, https://www.sans.org/cyber-security-courses/incident-response-planning.

"Incident Response Planning: 10 Steps to Success." CSO Online, 2021, https://www.csoonline.com/article/3240929/incident-response-planning-10-steps-to-success.html.

"The Importance of an Incident Response Plan." Dark Reading, 2021, https://www.darkreading.com/risk/the-importance-of-an-incident-response-plan/a/d-id/1334124.

Chapter 12

"Board Oversight of Cybersecurity: Key Considerations for Directors." Deloitte, 2021, https://www2.deloitte.com/us/en/insights/focus/cybersecurity/board-oversight-of-cybersecurity.html.

"Communicating Cybersecurity Risks and Incidents to the Board." SANS Institute, 2021, https://www.sans.org/reading-room/whitepapers/bestprac/communicating-cybersecurity-risks-incidents-board-38038.

"Measuring Cybersecurity Performance." National Institute of Standards and Technology, 2021, https://csrc.nist.gov/publications/detail/sp/800-55/rev-2/final.

Chapter 13

[1] Chen, X., & Hu, X. (2018). An overview of machine learning algorithms for intrusion detection. IEEE Access, 6, 58,186-58,200.

[2] Ghorbani, A., & Javanmardi, S. (2018). A review of machine learning techniques applied in network intrusion detection systems. Security and Communication Networks, 2018, 1-16.

[3] Lee, W., & Stolfo, S. (1998). A framework for constructing features and models for intrusion detection systems. ACM Transactions on Information and System Security, 1(1), 6-33.

[4] Zhang, Z., & Chen, Z. (2017). Machine learning in cyber security: A review of classification techniques and applications. Information Sciences, 413, 1-20.

[5] Bost, M., & Meunier, J. (2014). Machine learning applied to cybersecurity: A review of classification techniques and applications. In 2014 International Conference on Cyber Security and Protection of Digital Services (pp. 75-82). IEEE.

[6] Gao, L., & Chen, Z. (2018). A review of machine learning techniques applied in cyber security. IEEE Access, 6, 60,125-60,139.

[7] Zhang, Z., & Chen, Z. (2017). Machine learning in cyber security: A review of classification techniques and applications. Information Sciences, 413, 1-20.

[8] Lee, W., & Stolfo, S. (1998). A framework for constructing features and models for intrusion detection systems. ACM Transactions on Information and System Security, 1(1), 6-33.

[9] Ghorbani, A., & Javanmardi, S. (2018). A review of machine learning techniques applied in network intrusion detection systems. Security and Communication Networks, 2018, 1-16.

[10] Bost, M., & Meunier, J. (2014). Machine learning applied to cybersecurity: A review of classification techniques and applications.

In 2014 International Conference on Cyber Security and Protection of Digital Services (pp. 75-82). IEEE.

[11] Gao, L., & Chen, Z. (2018). A review of machine learning techniques applied in cyber security. IEEE Access, 6, 60,125-60,139.

[12] Zhang, Z., & Chen, Z. (2017). Machine learning in cyber security: A review of classification techniques and applications. Information Sciences, 413, 1-20.

[13] Barreno, M., Nelson, B., Sevcik, K., & Wallace, S. (2006). Can machine learning be secure? In 2006 IEEE Symposium on Security and Privacy (pp. 16-30). IEEE.

[14] Huber, M., & Wiederhold, G. (2018). Machine learning security: A review. ACM Computing Surveys, 51(4), 68.

[15] Gama, J., Zliobaite, I., Bifet, A., & Pechenizkiy, M. (2014). A survey on concept drift adaptation. ACM Computing Surveys, 46(4), 44.

[16] Bost, M., & Meunier, J. (2014). Machine learning applied to cybersecurity: A review of classification techniques and applications. In 2014 International Conference on Cyber Security and Protection of Digital Services (pp. 75-82). IEEE

Chapter 14

Certified Information Systems Security Professional (CISSP). (2021). About CISSP. Retrieved from https://www.isc2.org/cissp/about-cissp

Certified Ethical Hacker (CEH). (2021). About CEH. Retrieved from https://www.eccouncil.org/certification/certified-ethical-hacker/

Association of Computing Machinery. (2021). ACM Professional Membership. Retrieved from https://www.acm.org/professional-membership

International Association of Computer Science and Information Technology. (2021). IACSIT Membership. Retrieved from https://www.iacsit.org/membership

(ISC)². (2021). (ISC)² Community. Retrieved from https://www.isc2.org/community
SANS Institute. (2021). Cyber Security Training and Certification. Retrieved from https://www.sans.org/

(ISC)². (2021). Certified Cloud Security Professional (CCSP). Retrieved from https://www.isc2.org/ccsp/default.aspx

Appendix

Healthcare Information and Management Systems Society (HIMSS). (n.d.). Top 10 health IT security issues for 2017. Retrieved from https://www.himss.org/top-10-health-it-security-issues-2017

U.S. Department of Health and Human Services. (n.d.). Cybersecurity in the healthcare industry. Retrieved from https://www.hhs.gov/sites/default/files/cybersecurity-in-healthcare-industry.pdf

SANS Institute. (n.d.). Financial Institution Cybersecurity: Key Risks and Controls. Retrieved from https://www.sans.org/cyber-security-summit/archives/file/summit-archive-1530653381.pdf

National Institute of Standards and Technology (NIST). (2020). Cybersecurity for Financial Services: A Practical Guide. Retrieved from https://csrc.nist.gov/publications/detail/white-paper/2020/07/07/cybersecurity-for-financial-services-a-practical-guide/final

"Top Cybersecurity Risks for eCommerce Businesses" (https://www.securityinnovation.com/blog/top-cybersecurity-risks-for-ecommerce-businesses/)

"Top 10 Cybersecurity Risks for Technology Companies" (https://www.csoonline.com/article/3247834/top-10-cybersecurity-risks-for-technology-companies.html)

National Institute of Standards and Technology (NIST). (2020). Cybersecurity Framework. Retrieved from
https://www.nist.gov/cybersecurity-framework

U.S. Department of Homeland Security (DHS). (n.d.). Cybersecurity Risks and Best Practices. Retrieved from
https://www.dhs.gov/cybersecurity-risks-and-best-practices

"Top 10 Cybersecurity Risks for the Financial Services Industry" (https://www.forbes.com/sites/forbestechcouncil/2018/01/16/top-10-cybersecurity-risks-for-the-financial-services-industry/?sh=3e6928d05d7a)

"5 Cybersecurity Risks Facing Fintech Companies" (https://www.investopedia.com/terms/f/fintech-risk.asp)